THE BEST OF

Waffles &
Pancakes

THE BEST OF

Waffles & Pancakes

A COOKBOOK

Jane Stacey

Food Photography by Elizabeth Watt

CollinsPublishersSanFrancisco
A Division of HarperCollinsPublishers

First published in USA 1994 by CollinsPublishersSanFrancisco
1160 Battery Street, San Francisco, CA 94111

Produced by Smallwood and Stewart, Inc.,
New York City

© 1994 Smallwood and Stewart, Inc.

Editor: Kathy Kingsley
Food Styling: Dora Jonassen
Prop Styling: Susan Byrnes

Food Styling for p. 89: Louise Burbidge

Photography credits: Arthur Hustwit/Leo de Wys Inc.: p. 1.
Susanna Pashko/Envision: p. 7. Lynn Karlin: p. 11. Robert Holmes: p. 19.
Mathias Oppersdorff: p. 37. Jacqui Hurst: p. 61. Boys Syndication: p. 67.
Tim Gibson/Envision: p. 81.

Library of Congress Cataloging-in-Publication Data

Stacey, Jane
    The best of waffles & pancakes: a cookbook/Jane Stacey;
food photography by Elizabeth Watt.
        p.   cm.
    Includes index.
    ISBN 0-00-255475-5
    1. Pancakes, Waffles, etc.   I. Title. II. Title: Best of waffles
and pancakes.
TX770.P34S73   1994
641.8'15—dc20   94-17339
                                                                 CIP

Printed in China

Contents

Introduction

Thousands of years have passed since man first learned that adding water to crushed grain and heating the mixture on a flat surface would produce a delicious breadlike food. With the discovery of leavening and honey and other sweeteners, the pancake's place in almost every culture's cuisine was assured. In China, the pancakes are rolled thin by hand, steamed, stuffed with meat or vegetables, and folded for serving. In Japan, they are studded with chopped oysters and served with a hot chile dipping sauce. South Africa and Bulgaria both have pumpkin pancakes; Finland boasts a baked version with shredded carrots, eggs, and cream. The potato pancake is truly international: In Ireland it is the boxty, in France the pachade, in Switzerland the röesti, in Eastern Europe the latke.

With the availability of a wide variety of grains, flours, and dairy products and year-round fresh fruits and vegetables, we need not be

Crêpe stand, Boulder

limited when it comes to creating waffles and pancakes. Once considered only breakfast fare, they can now be served at any time of day as snacks, side dishes, main courses, and desserts. The recipes that follow offer all the classic dishes and some surprising new inventions as well. By all means treasure those blueberry pancakes you loved as a child, but do try a tiny potato pancake with a dollop of sour cream as an hors d'oeuvre or herbed waffles with chicken salad for your next luncheon. At dinner, replace the usual side dish of rice with a wild rice pancake, ginger and carrot skillet pancake, or a chunky sweet corn cake. Onion cheddar waffles and curried corn waffles are great for a snack and are perfect as sandwich material. And ultrathin crêpes, surprisingly easy to make, provide a light and interesting wrapping for all kinds of fillings, both sweet and savory.

For lovers of sweets, pancakes and waffles are endlessly versatile. Spread with butter and sprinkled with sugar or drizzled with honey and cinnamon, plain crêpes, pear-almond waffles, or honey-hazelnut pancakes deliciously complement coffee any time of the day. A more luxuriant fare of mocha waffles, chocolate crêpes, or panettone pancakes will make a perfect finale to even the most formal dinner party.

Many of us treasure childhood memories of waking to the warm, yeasty smell of pancakes on Sunday morning, or marveling at perfectly patterned squares of waffles on our dinner plate. My hope is that the recipes in this book will inspire you to re-create those wonderful moments any time the spirit moves you.

Jane Stacey

NOTE: All of the following recipes were tested with unsalted butter, large eggs, heavy cream, whole milk, sugar, and honey. If necessary they can be modified easily for dietary considerations. Low-fat or skim milk can be substituted for whole milk, half-and-half, or sour cream, and toppings made of heavy cream or sour cream can be replaced with low-fat sour cream or nonfat yogurt. In many cases, especially with waffles, egg yolks can be omitted, since the whipped egg whites will keep the waffle light and the lower fat content will keep it crisp. The melted butter called for by most of the recipes can be replaced by melted margarine or vegetable oil and can be reduced to one tablespoon.

Buttermilk Waffles

*If you want to accommodate a crowd, try serving these with a choice of toppings
such as sliced fruit, jam, chopped nuts, or flavored yogurt.*

1 cup all-purpose flour

1 cup whole-wheat flour

¼ cup packed light brown sugar

1 teaspoon baking soda

½ teaspoon cinnamon

¼ teaspoon freshly grated
nutmeg

¼ teaspoon salt

1½ cups buttermilk

2 large eggs, separated, at room
temperature

½ cup (1 stick) butter, melted

2 tablespoons honey

Butter & maple syrup, for topping

Preheat the oven to 200°F. Preheat a waffle iron. In a medium-size bowl, combine both flours, brown sugar, baking soda, cinnamon, nutmeg, and salt.

In another medium-size bowl, whisk together the buttermilk, egg yolks, butter, and honey. Pour this mixture into the dry ingredients, stirring with a few quick strokes to form a lumpy batter.

In a small bowl, using an electric mixer set at high, beat the egg whites until stiff peaks form. Using a rubber spatula, gently and thoroughly fold the egg whites into the batter.

Lightly grease or spray the grids of the waffle iron. Follow the manufacturer's instructions, or spoon about ⅓ cup batter (amount varies with size of iron) onto the hot iron and spread it almost to the corners of the grids. Close the lid and bake for 1½ to 2 minutes, or until the waffles are golden brown, their edges look dry, and they do not stick to the grids. Transfer the waffles to the oven, placing them directly on the rack so they will stay crisp. Repeat with the remaining batter.

Transfer the waffles to warmed serving plates and top each serving with butter and syrup. **Makes 8 to 10 waffles.**

Beekeeping, Maine

Cornmeal Waffles with Fresh Peach Topping

Yellow cornmeal not only gives these waffles a sweet taste and crunchy texture but also makes them sturdy enough for freezing and reheating. Individually wrap cooled waffles in plastic wrap and freeze for up to 1 month. Reheat unwrapped waffles in a toaster or conventional oven.

Fresh Peach Topping:

3 ripe medium peaches, peeled, pitted & sliced

2 tablespoons honey

2 teaspoons fresh lemon juice

1 teaspoon grated lemon zest

Cornmeal Waffles:

1 cup yellow cornmeal

1 cup all-purpose flour

1 tablespoon granulated sugar

¾ teaspoon baking powder

¾ teaspoon baking soda

1 cup buttermilk

3 large eggs, separated, at room temperature

3 tablespoons butter, melted

Confectioners' sugar, for dusting

Thin strips lemon zest, for decoration (optional)

Prepare the topping: In a medium-size bowl, combine all of the ingredients for the topping. Let stand at room temperature for 30 minutes, or until ready to serve.

Prepare the waffles: Preheat the oven to 200°F. Preheat a waffle iron. In a medium-size bowl, combine the cornmeal, flour, granulated sugar, baking powder, and baking soda.

In a small bowl, whisk together the buttermilk, egg yolks, and butter. Pour this mixture into the dry ingredients, stirring with a few quick strokes to form a lumpy batter.

In a medium-size bowl, using an electric mixer set at high, beat the egg whites until stiff peaks form. Using a rubber spatula, gently and thoroughly

fold the egg whites into the batter.

Lightly grease or spray the grids of the waffle iron. Follow the manufacturer's instructions, or spoon about ⅓ cup batter (amount varies with size of iron) onto the hot iron and spread it almost to the corners of the grids. Close the lid and bake for 2 to 3 minutes, or until the waffles are golden brown, their edges look dry, and they do not stick to the grids. Transfer the baked waffles to the oven, placing them directly on the rack so they will stay crisp. Repeat with the remaining batter.

Transfer the waffles to warmed serving plates and top each serving with the peaches. Dust with confectioners' sugar and decorate with lemon zest, if desired. **Makes 6 to 8 waffles.**

Lemon Waffles with Blackberries

There's plenty of lemon flavor in these slightly sweet, cakelike waffles. Their pale yellow color contrasts beautifully with the deep purple blackberries. Fresh berries are best, but frozen or canned can be substituted. Set out additional lemon-flavored yogurt or unsweetened whipped cream to serve with the waffles.

Blackberry Topping:

2½ cups fresh blackberries

2 tablespoons granulated sugar

Lemon Waffles:

2 cups all-purpose flour

¼ cup granulated sugar

1½ teaspoons baking powder

½ teaspoon baking soda

1 cup lemon-flavored yogurt

¾ cup milk

2 large eggs, at room temperature

5 tablespoons butter, melted

2 teaspoons grated lemon zest

Confectioners' sugar, for dusting (optional)

Prepare the topping: Place the blackberries in a medium-size nonreactive bowl. Sprinkle the granulated sugar over them and stir gently to combine. Using a wooden spoon, mash the berries to bring out their juice. Let stand at room temperature until ready to serve.

Prepare the waffles: Preheat the oven to 200°F. Preheat a waffle iron. In a medium-size bowl, combine the flour, granulated sugar, baking powder, and baking soda. In another medium-size bowl, whisk together the yogurt, milk, eggs, butter, and lemon zest. Pour this mixture into the dry ingredients, stirring to form a smooth batter.

Lightly grease or spray the grids of the waffle iron. Follow the manufacturer's instructions, or spoon about ⅓ cup of batter (amount varies with size of iron) onto the hot iron and spread it almost to the corners of the grids. Close the lid

and bake for 2 to 3 minutes, or until the waffles are golden brown, their edges look dry, and they do not stick to the grids. Transfer the baked waffles to the oven, placing them directly on the rack so they will stay crisp. Repeat with the remaining batter.

Transfer the waffles to serving plates and top each serving with the blackberries. Dust with confectioners' sugar, if desired. **Makes 8 to 10 waffles.**

Belgian Waffles with Strawberries & Cream

Belgian waffles became popular during the 1964 World's Fair in New York, where they were served topped with fresh strawberries and whipped cream, as they are here.

Strawberry Topping:

4 cups sliced strawberries

½ cup fresh orange juice

1 teaspoon sugar

Belgian Waffles:

1 cup cake flour

½ cup all-purpose flour

2 tablespoons sugar

1½ teaspoons baking powder

¾ teaspoon baking soda

1½ cups sour cream

3 large eggs, separated, at room temperature

3 tablespoons butter, melted

Seeds of 1 vanilla bean or 1 teaspoon pure vanilla extract

Cream Topping:

1 cup heavy cream

½ teaspoon pure vanilla extract

Prepare the strawberry topping: In a medium-size nonreactive bowl, combine the strawberries, orange juice, and sugar. Let stand at room temperature until ready to use.

Prepare the waffles: Preheat the oven to 200°F. Preheat a Belgian waffle iron. In a medium-size bowl, sift together both flours, the sugar, baking powder, and baking soda.

In another medium-size bowl, whisk together the sour cream, egg yolks, butter, and vanilla bean seeds. Pour this mixture into the dry ingredients, stirring with a few quick strokes to form a lumpy batter.

In another medium-size bowl, using an electric mixer set at high, beat the egg whites until stiff peaks form. Using a rubber spatula, gently and thoroughly fold the egg whites into the batter.

Lightly grease or spray the grids of the waffle iron. Follow the manufacturer's instructions, or spoon about ⅓ cup batter (amount varies with size of iron) onto the hot iron and spread it almost to the corners of the grids. Close the lid and bake for 1 to 2 minutes, or until the waffles are golden brown, their edges look dry, and they do not stick to the grids. Transfer the baked waffles to the oven, placing them directly on the rack so they will stay crisp. Repeat with the remaining batter.

Prepare the cream topping: In a medium-size bowl, using an electric mixer set at medium-high, beat the cream with the vanilla until stiff peaks form.

Transfer the waffles to warmed serving plates and top each serving with the strawberries and whipped cream. **Makes 8 to 10 waffles.**

Whole-Wheat Sourdough Waffles

These waffles have everything going for them ~ the whole-grain richness of whole wheat, the tang of sourdough, and the spicy sweetness of cinnamon and raisins. Drizzle them with maple syrup and serve with grilled slices of smoked ham and chunks of fresh pineapple on the side for a Sunday morning feast. For a variation, add 1 tablespoon grated orange zest and ¼ cup chopped walnuts to the batter.

I cup whole-wheat flour

¾ cup all-purpose flour

I teaspoon baking powder

½ teaspoon cinnamon

¼ teaspoon salt

½ cup raisins

I cup milk

¾ cup sourdough starter (p. 57)

2 large eggs, separated, at room temperature

5 tablespoons butter, melted

I tablespoon honey

Butter & maple syrup, for topping

Preheat the oven to 200°F. Preheat a waffle iron. In a medium-size bowl, combine both flours, the baking powder, cinnamon, salt, and raisins.

In another medium-size bowl, whisk together the milk, sourdough starter, egg yolks, butter, and honey. Pour this mixture into the dry ingredients, stirring with a few quick strokes to form a lumpy batter.

In a small bowl, using an electric mixer set at high, beat the egg whites until stiff peaks form. Using a rubber spatula, gently and thoroughly fold the egg whites into the batter.

Lightly grease or spray the grids of the waffle iron. Follow the manufacturer's instructions, or spoon about ⅓ cup batter (amount varies with size of iron) onto the hot iron and spread it almost to the corners of the grids. Close the lid and bake for 1½ to 2 minutes, or until the waffles

Maple-syrup making, Maine

are lightly browned, their edges look dry, and they do not stick to the grids. Transfer the baked waffles to the oven, placing them directly on the rack so they will stay crisp. Repeat with the remaining batter.

Transfer the waffles to warmed serving plates and top each serving with butter and syrup. **Makes 8 to 10 waffles.**

Apple-Oatmeal Waffles with Spiced Fruit

*The whole oats remain slightly chewy in these apple-scented waffles.
The spiced fruit topping can be made ahead and served at room
temperature or reheated just before serving. For a refreshing, tangy flavor,
spoon a dollop of plain yogurt over the fruit.*

Spiced Fruit Topping:

2 large cooking apples such as
Granny Smith, peeled, cored
& cut into ¼-inch slices

2 large pears such as Bartlett or
Bosc, peeled, cored & cut
into ¼-inch slices

1 cup apple cider or apple juice

½ cup dried apple slices, chopped

⅓ cup packed light brown sugar

¼ cup raisins

1 teaspoon cinnamon

½ teaspoon freshly grated nutmeg

⅛ teaspoon allspice

Apple-Oatmeal Waffles:

1 cup all-purpose flour

1 cup rolled oats

2 tablespoons light brown sugar

1 teaspoon baking powder

½ teaspoon baking soda

1 cup milk

3 large eggs, at room
temperature

½ cup applesauce

3 tablespoons butter, melted

Prepare the topping: In a medium-size saucepan, combine all of the topping ingredients. Bring the mixture to a boil over medium-high heat, stirring occasionally. Reduce the heat to medium and cook, stirring frequently, for 12 to 15 minutes, or until the fruit is tender but not mushy and the juices have thickened slightly. Remove the pan from the heat and keep warm.

20

Prepare the waffles: Preheat the oven to 200°F. Preheat a waffle iron. In a medium-size bowl, combine the flour, oats, brown sugar, baking powder, and baking soda.

In another medium-size bowl, whisk together the milk, eggs, applesauce, and butter. Add this mixture to the dry ingredients, stirring to form a smooth batter.

Lightly grease or spray the grids of the waffle iron. Follow the manufacturer's instructions, or spoon about ⅓ cup batter (amount varies with size of iron) onto the hot iron and spread it almost to the corners of the grids. Close the lid and bake for 2 to 3 minutes, or until the waffles are golden brown, their edges look dry, and they do not stick to the grids. Transfer the baked waffles to the oven, placing them directly on the rack so they will stay crisp. Repeat with the remaining batter.

Transfer the waffles to warmed serving plates and top each serving with the spiced fruit. **Makes 8 to 10 waffles.**

Yogurt Waffles with Melon & Mint

Enjoy this waffle combination in the summer months, when mint is plentiful and melons are at their peak. Cantaloupe or honeydew is called for in this recipe, but there are dozens of other varieties to choose from such as Crenshaw, which has fragrant, salmon-colored flesh and a rich, spicy taste, or delicately sweet Persian with its orange-pink flesh.

Melon:

- 1 ripe medium cantaloupe or honeydew melon, peeled, seeded & cut into 1-inch pieces or scooped into balls
- 2 tablespoons fresh lime juice
- 1 tablespoon chopped fresh mint

Yogurt Waffles:

- 2 cups all-purpose flour
- 2 tablespoons sugar
- 1½ teaspoons baking powder
- ½ teaspoon baking soda
- ¼ teaspoon freshly grated nutmeg
- 1¾ cups plain yogurt
- 2 large eggs, separated, at room temperature
- 3 tablespoons butter, melted
- Plain yogurt, for topping (optional)

Prepare the melon: In a medium-size bowl, combine the melon, lime juice, and mint. Cover with plastic wrap and chill until ready to use.

Prepare the waffles: Preheat the oven to 200°F. Preheat a waffle iron. In a large bowl, combine the flour, sugar, baking powder, baking soda, and nutmeg.

In a medium-size bowl, whisk together the yogurt, egg yolks, and butter. Pour this mixture into the dry ingredients, stirring with a few quick strokes to form a lumpy batter.

In a small bowl, using an electric

mixer set at high, beat the egg whites until stiff peaks form. Using a rubber spatula, gently and thoroughly fold the egg whites into the batter.

Lightly grease or spray the grids of the waffle iron. Follow the manufacturer's instructions, or spoon about ⅓ cup batter (amount varies with size of iron) onto the hot iron and spread it almost to the corners of the grids. Close the lid and bake for 1 to 2 minutes, or until the waffles are golden brown, their edges look dry, and they do not stick to the grids. Transfer the baked waffles to the oven, placing them directly on the rack so they will stay crisp. Repeat with the remaining batter.

Transfer the waffles to warmed serving plates and top each serving with yogurt, if desired. Serve the melon as a topping or on the side. **Makes 8 to 10 waffles.**

Poppy Seed Waffles with Lemon Cream

These waffles, golden on the outside and tender inside, are luscious topped with tart, silky Lemon Cream, or a scoop of vanilla ice cream.

Lemon Cream:

1 large egg

2 large egg yolks

⅓ cup sugar

½ cup fresh lemon juice

1 tablespoon grated lemon zest

1 cup heavy cream

Poppy Seed Waffles:

1 cup all-purpose flour

1 cup cake flour

½ cup sugar

¾ teaspoon baking powder

½ teaspoon baking soda

2 tablespoons poppy seeds

1 cup sour cream

½ cup milk

3 large eggs, separated, at room temperature

4 tablespoons (½ stick) butter, melted

½ teaspoon pure almond extract

Prepare the lemon cream: In a medium-size bowl, whisk together the egg, egg yolks, and sugar. Slowly add the lemon juice, whisking until well blended. Transfer the mixture to a medium-size saucepan and cook over medium heat, whisking constantly, for 8 to 10 minutes, or until the mixture begins to thicken. Remove the pan from the heat and stir in the lemon zest. Transfer the mixture to a shallow bowl and let cool to room temperature. Refrigerate for 2 hours, or until thoroughly chilled.

In another medium-size bowl, using an electric mixer set at high, beat the cream until soft peaks form. Using a rubber spatula, gently and thoroughly fold the whipped cream into the lemon mixture.

Refrigerate until ready to serve.

Prepare the waffles: Preheat the oven to 200°F. Preheat a waffle iron. In a medium-size bowl, sift together both flours, the sugar, baking powder, and baking soda. Stir in the poppy seeds.

In another medium-size bowl, whisk together the sour cream, milk, egg yolks, butter, and almond extract. Pour this mixture into the dry ingredients, stirring with a few quick strokes to form a lumpy batter.

In another medium-size bowl, using an electric mixer set at high, beat the egg whites until stiff peaks form. Using a rubber spatula, gently and thoroughly fold the egg whites into the batter.

Lightly grease or spray the grids of the waffle iron. Follow the manufacturer's instructions, or spoon about ⅓ cup batter (amount varies with size of iron) onto the hot iron and spread it almost to the corners of the grids. Close the lid and bake for 2 to 3 minutes, or until the waffles are golden brown, the edges look dry, and they do not stick to the grids. Transfer the waffles to the oven, placing them directly on the rack so they will stay crisp. Repeat with the remaining batter.

Transfer the waffles to warmed serving plates and top each serving with lemon cream. **Makes 8 to 10 waffles.**

Pear-Almond Waffles

*The flavors of pears and almonds have a natural affinity for one another
and create a perfect breakfast waffle. An extra-ripe pear in the batter
will make the waffles even sweeter. Serve the waffles topped with maple syrup or
maple cream (whipped maple syrup, available in specialty food shops).*

2 cups all-purpose flour

½ cup toasted ground almonds

⅓ cup sugar

1¾ teaspoons baking powder

½ teaspoon baking soda

¼ teaspoon salt

1¼ cups milk

3 large eggs, separated, at room
temperature

3 tablespoons butter, melted

½ teaspoon pure almond
extract

1 ripe medium pear such as
Bartlett or Bosc, peeled,
cored & chopped

Maple syrup or maple cream,
for topping

Sliced fresh pears, for
decoration (optional)

Preheat the oven to 200°F. Preheat a waffle iron. In a medium-size bowl, combine the flour, almonds, sugar, baking powder, baking soda, and salt.

In another medium-size bowl, whisk together the milk, egg yolks, butter, and almond extract. Pour this mixture into the dry ingredients, stirring with a few quick strokes to form a lumpy batter. Stir in the chopped pear.

In another medium-size bowl, using an electric mixer set at high, beat the egg whites until stiff peaks form. Using a rubber spatula, gently and thoroughly fold the egg whites into the batter.

Lightly spray or grease the grids of the waffle iron. Follow the manufacturer's instructions, or spoon about ⅓ cup batter (amount varies with size of iron) onto the hot iron and spread it almost to the corners of the grids. Close the lid and bake for 2 to 3 minutes, or until the

waffles are golden brown, their edges look dry, and they do not stick to the grids. Transfer the waffles to the oven, placing them directly on the rack so they will stay crisp. Repeat with the remaining batter.

Transfer the waffles to warmed serving plates and top each serving with maple syrup. Decorate with pears slices, if desired. **Makes 6 to 8 waffles.**

Sour Cream Waffles with Walnut Butter & Cherries

This waffle is tender and creamy thanks to the addition of sour cream. For extra cherry flavor, add ⅓ cup of finely chopped dried cherries to the batter or the cherry topping (or both). Their chewy texture and rich, sweet-tart taste are absolutely irresistible.

Walnut Butter:

¼ cup chopped walnuts

½ cup (1 stick) unsalted butter, softened

2 tablespoons confectioners' sugar

1 tablespoon walnut oil

Cherry Topping:

2 cups canned sweet cherries, drained

¼ cup light corn syrup

3 tablespoons granulated sugar

1 tablespoon cornstarch

1 tablespoon fresh lemon juice

1 teaspoon pure vanilla extract

Sour Cream Waffles:

2 cups all-purpose flour

3 tablespoons granulated sugar

1½ teaspoons baking powder

½ teaspoon baking soda

1¾ cups sour cream

2 large eggs, separated, at room temperature

3 tablespoons butter, melted

2 teaspoons pure vanilla extract

Prepare the walnut butter: Place the walnuts in a small skillet and toast over medium-high heat, stirring frequently, for 2 to 3 minutes, or until they begin to brown. Remove the pan from the heat and let cool slightly.

In a food processor fitted with the metal blade, combine the toasted walnuts, butter, confectioners' sugar, and oil, and process for 5 seconds. Scrape down

the sides of the bowl and process again for 3 to 5 seconds, or until the ingredients are well blended.

Scrape the butter onto a sheet of waxed paper. Wrap the butter in the waxed paper, shaping it into a cylinder about 10 inches long and 1 inch in diameter. Chill until ready to serve.

Prepare the topping: In a medium-size saucepan, combine all of the topping ingredients and stir to dissolve the cornstarch. Bring the mixture to a boil over medium-high heat, stirring occasionally. Transfer the mixture to a medium-size bowl and let stand at room temperature until ready to use.

Prepare the waffles: Preheat the oven to 200°F. Preheat a waffle iron. In a medium-size bowl, combine the flour, granulated sugar, baking powder, and baking soda.

In another medium-size bowl, whisk together the sour cream, egg yolks, butter, and vanilla. Pour this mixture into the dry ingredients, stirring with a few quick strokes to form a lumpy batter.

In a small bowl, using an electric mixer set at high, beat the egg whites until stiff peaks form. Using a rubber spatula, gently and thoroughly fold the egg whites into the batter.

Lightly grease or spray the grids of the waffle iron. Follow the manufacturer's instructions, or spoon about ⅓ cup batter (amount varies with size of iron) onto the hot iron and spread it almost to the corners of the grids. Close the lid and bake for 2 to 3 minutes, or until the waffles are golden brown, their edges look dry, and they do not stick to the grids. Transfer the waffles to the oven, placing them directly on the rack so they will stay crisp. Repeat with the remaining batter.

Unwrap the walnut butter and cut into ¼-inch-thick slices. Transfer the waffles to warmed serving plates and top each serving with walnut butter and cherry topping. **Makes 8 to 10 waffles.**

Mocha Waffles with Mascarpone

Serve these coffee-flavored dessert waffles hot so the rum-scented mascarpone cream melts slightly. Mascarpone is an Italian triple cream cheese. If unavailable, ice cream, frozen yogurt, or whipped cream can be used instead of the topping.

Mascarpone Topping:

1 cup heavy cream

½ cup mascarpone

3 tablespoons granulated sugar

2 tablespoons dark rum

Mocha Waffles:

¾ cup all-purpose flour

¾ cup cake flour

¾ cup nonalkalized un-
sweetened cocoa powder

¾ cup granulated sugar

1 ½ teaspoons baking powder

½ teaspoon baking soda

2 tablespoons instant coffee
powder

¼ cup hot freshly brewed coffee

2 ounces unsweetened
chocolate, melted

5 tablespoons butter, melted

1 ¼ cups sour cream

3 large eggs, at room temperature

1 teaspoon pure vanilla extract

Cocoa & confectioners' sugar, for
decoration (optional)

Fresh raspberries, for decoration
(optional)

Prepare the topping: In a medium-size bowl, using an electric mixer set at high, beat the cream until soft peaks form. Add the mascarpone, granulated sugar, and rum, and beat for 15 to 30 seconds, or until the mixture is well blended and stiff. Cover with plastic wrap and chill until ready to serve. (It can be made 3 to 4 hours ahead.)

Prepare the waffles: Preheat the oven to 200°F. Preheat a waffle iron. In a medium-size bowl, sift together both flours, the cocoa powder, granulated sugar, baking powder, and baking soda.

In a small bowl, dissolve the instant coffee in the brewed coffee. Stir in the

chocolate and butter.

In another medium-size bowl, whisk together the sour cream, eggs, and vanilla. Pour this mixture and the coffee mixture into the dry ingredients, stirring to form a smooth batter.

Lightly grease or spray the grids of the waffle iron. Follow the manufacturer's instructions, or spoon about ⅓ cup batter (amount varies with size of iron) onto the hot iron and spread it almost to the corners of the grids. Close the lid and bake for about 1 minute, or until the edges are set (they will not be crisp) and they do not stick to the grids. Transfer the baked waffles to a baking sheet or ovenproof platter and keep warm in the oven. Repeat with the remaining batter.

Transfer the waffles to warmed plates and top each serving with the mascarpone cream. Dust with cocoa and confectioners' sugar and serve with raspberries, if desired. **Makes 8 to 10 waffles.**

Raspberry Puree & Sorbet Topping: In a food processor fitted with the metal blade, combine 2 pints fresh raspberries or two 12-ounce bags frozen raspberries, thawed, and 2 tablespoons confectioners' sugar; process until pureed. Strain the puree through a medium-fine sieve set over a medium-size bowl; discard the seeds. Stir in 2 teaspoons lemon juice. Serve the waffles at room temperature, topping each serving with a scoop of store-bought raspberry sorbet and 3 tablespoons of the raspberry puree.

Banana, Coconut & Chocolate Topping: In a small skillet, toast ½ cup flaked coconut over medium heat, stirring frequently, for 2 to 3 minutes, or until golden brown. Remove the skillet from the heat and set aside. In a medium-size skillet over medium heat, melt 4 tablespoons unsalted butter. Stir in 3 tablespoons dark brown sugar. Add 3 ripe medium-size bananas, sliced, and cook, stirring frequently, for about 3 to 4 minutes, or until softened. Serve the waffles warm, topping each serving with the sliced bananas. Drizzle with store-bought hot fudge or chocolate sauce and decorate with the toasted coconut.

Caramel-Pecan Waffles

*Toasted pecans appear twice in this fabulous sundae-like dessert.
They are added to the rich warm sauce and folded into the cinnamon-scented
waffle batter to create a satisfying taste sensation accented by
smooth and creamy vanilla ice cream. This is a treat for adults and kids alike.*

Caramel-Pecan Sauce:

1 cup granulated sugar

1 cup heavy cream

2 tablespoons light corn syrup

3 tablespoons butter

2 teaspoons pure vanilla extract

¾ cup toasted chopped pecans

Pecan Waffles:

1½ cups all-purpose flour

½ cup packed dark brown sugar

½ cup toasted chopped pecans

1½ teaspoons baking powder

¾ teaspoon baking soda

½ teaspoon cinnamon

1 cup sour cream

¾ cup milk

3 large eggs, separated, at room temperature

3 tablespoons butter, melted

1 pint vanilla ice cream, for topping

Prepare the sauce: In a medium-size heavy saucepan over medium-high heat, cook the granulated sugar without stirring for about 1 to 2 minutes, or until it melts and is just beginning to color. Reduce the heat to medium and cook, stirring constantly, for 1½ to 2 minutes, or until all the sugar is melted and it becomes a clear golden color. Remove the pan from the heat and add the cream in a slow steady stream, stirring carefully until well blended. (The caramel will bubble and steam as you add the cream. If it stiffens, return the saucepan to medium heat and cook, stirring constantly, until smooth and melted.) Stir in the corn syrup, butter, and vanilla until well blended. Stir in the pecans. Keep warm.

Prepare the waffles: Preheat the oven to 200°F. Preheat a waffle iron. In a medium-size bowl, combine the flour, brown sugar, pecans, baking powder, baking soda, and cinnamon.

In another medium-size bowl, whisk together the sour cream, milk, egg yolks, and butter. Pour this mixture into the dry ingredients, stirring with a few quick strokes to form a lumpy batter.

In another medium-size bowl, using an electric mixer set at high, beat the egg whites until stiff peaks form. Using a rubber spatula, gently and thoroughly fold the egg whites into the batter.

Lightly spray or grease the grids of the waffle iron. Follow the manufacturer's instructions, or spoon about ⅓ cup batter (amount varies with size of iron) onto the hot iron and spread it almost to the corners of the grids. Close the lid and bake for 2 to 3 minutes, or until the waffles are golden brown, their edges look dry, and they do not stick to the grids. Transfer the baked waffles to the oven, placing them directly on the rack so they will stay crisp. Repeat with the remaining batter.

Transfer the waffles to warmed serving plates and top each serving with a scoop of ice cream and warm caramel-pecan sauce. **Makes 8 to 10 waffles.**

Cheddar & Onion Waffles with Chutney

This slightly crisp waffle is chock-full of sautéed onion. The beer adds an interesting flavor and pairs naturally with the sharp Cheddar. Cut in quarters and topped with a dollop of chutney or your favorite salsa, these waffles are perfect for a casual brunch or weekend treat.

2 tablespoons butter
1 medium onion, finely chopped
1¾ cups all-purpose flour
1 teaspoon baking powder
½ teaspoon baking soda
¼ teaspoon freshly grated nutmeg

½ cup beer
½ cup milk
2 large eggs, separated, at room temperature
1 cup sharp Cheddar cheese, shredded
1 cup prepared chutney, for topping

Preheat the oven to 200°F. Preheat a waffle iron. In a small skillet over medium heat, melt the butter. Add the onions and cook, stirring frequently, for 2 to 3 minutes, or until softened. Remove the pan from the heat.

In a medium-size bowl, combine the flour, baking powder, baking soda, and nutmeg. In a small bowl, whisk together the beer, milk, and egg yolks. Pour this mixture into the dry ingredients, stirring with a few quick strokes to form a lumpy batter. Add the onions and cheese, stirring until just blended.

In another small bowl, using an electric mixer set at high, beat the egg whites until stiff peaks form. Using a rubber spatula, gently and thoroughly fold the egg whites into the batter.

Lightly grease or spray the grids of the waffle iron. Follow the manufacturer's instructions, or spoon about ⅓ cup batter

English cheese shop

(amount varies with size of iron) onto the hot iron and spread it almost to the corners of the grids. Close the lid and bake for 2 to 3 minutes, or until the waffles are golden brown, their edges look dry, and they do not stick to the grids. Transfer the waffles to the oven, placing them directly on the rack so they will stay crisp. Repeat with the remaining batter.

Cut each waffle diagonally into 4 triangles. Spoon some chutney into the center of each serving plate and arrange the waffles around it. **Makes 6 to 8 waffles.**

Bacon, Cheddar & Onion Waffles: Prepare the waffle batter as directed, adding ½ cup cooked crumbled bacon to the batter along with the onion and cheese. Bake and serve as directed.

Apple, Potato & Sausage Waffles

A highly spiced breakfast sausage accents the sweet apple and mild potato flavors of these thick and substantial waffles. Try them for breakfast with just a drizzle of maple syrup and a glass of fresh-squeezed orange juice.

1 ½ cups all-purpose flour

1 ½ teaspoons baking powder

½ teaspoon baking soda

¼ teaspoon salt

1 cup milk

3 large eggs, separated, at room temperature

2 tablespoons butter, melted

6 ounces cooked pork or turkey breakfast sausage, crumbled

½ cup peeled, chopped, cooked potatoes

½ cup peeled, grated apple

Maple syrup, for topping

Chopped apples, for topping

Preheat the oven to 200°F. Preheat a waffle iron. In a medium-size bowl, combine the flour, baking powder, baking soda, and salt.

In a small bowl, whisk together the milk, egg yolks, and butter. Pour this mixture into the dry ingredients, stirring with a few quick strokes to form a lumpy batter. Stir in the sausage, potatoes, and apples.

In another medium-size bowl, using an electric mixer set at high, beat the egg whites until stiff peaks form. Using a rubber spatula, gently and thoroughly fold the egg whites into the batter.

Lightly spray or grease the grids of the waffle iron. Follow the manufacturer's instructions, or spoon about ⅓ cup batter (amount varies with size of iron) onto the hot iron and spread it almost to the corners of the grids. Close the lid and bake for 2 to 3 minutes, or until the

waffles are golden brown, their edges look dry, and they do not stick to the grids. Transfer the waffles to the oven, placing them directly on the rack so they will stay crisp. Repeat with the remaining batter.

Transfer the waffles to warmed serving plates and top each serving with syrup and apples. **Makes 8 to 10 waffles.**

Semolina Waffles with Red Pepper–Basil Butter

Semolina, milled from hard durum wheat, forms the base of most pastas. Added to waffles, it imparts a creamy yellow color and slightly nutty flavor. It is sold in Italian markets, health food stores, and some large supermarkets.

Red Pepper–Basil Butter:

½ cup (1 stick) butter, softened

3 tablespoons finely chopped red bell pepper

1 tablespoon minced fresh basil leaves

1 garlic clove, minced

Semolina Waffles:

1 cup semolina

¾ cup all-purpose flour

1 tablespoon sesame seeds (optional)

1¾ teaspoons baking powder

½ teaspoon baking soda

¼ teaspoon salt

1¼ cups milk

2 large eggs, separated, at room temperature

3 tablespoons butter, melted

Fresh basil leaves, for garnish (optional)

Prepare the butter: In a food processor fitted with the metal blade, combine the butter, bell pepper, basil, and garlic, and process for 5 seconds. Scrape down the sides of the bowl and process for 3 to 5 seconds more, or until the ingredients are well blended.

Scrape the butter onto a sheet of waxed paper. Wrap the butter in the waxed paper, shaping it into a cylinder about 10 inches long and 1 inch in diameter. Chill until ready to serve.

Prepare the waffles: Preheat the oven to 200°F. Preheat a waffle iron. In a medium-size bowl, combine the semolina, flour, sesame seeds if desired, baking

powder, baking soda, and salt.

In a small bowl, whisk together the milk, egg yolks, and butter. Pour this mixture into the dry ingredients, stirring with a few quick strokes to form a lumpy batter.

In another small bowl, using an electric mixer set at high, beat the egg whites until stiff peaks form. Using a rubber spatula, gently and thoroughly fold the egg whites into the batter.

Lightly spray or grease the grids of the waffle iron. Follow the manufacturer's instructions, or spoon about ⅓ cup batter (amount varies with size of iron) onto the hot iron and spread it almost to the corners of the grids. Close the lid and bake for 2 to 3 minutes, or until the waffles are golden brown, their edges look dry, and they do not stick to the grids. Transfer the waffles to the oven, placing them directly on the rack so they will stay crisp. Repeat with the remaining batter.

Unwrap the butter and cut into ¼-inch-thick slices. Transfer the waffles to warmed serving plates and top each serving with the red pepper–basil butter. Garnish with basil leaves, if desired. **Makes 6 to 8 waffles.**

Herbed Waffles & Chicken Salad

*Chicken salad is studded with seedless grapes and combined
with herbed waffles in this attractive luncheon presentation. To save time,
prepare the salad and waffles ahead, then reheat the waffles in a
350°F oven for about 10 minutes before serving. To complete the dish, serve
with chilled asparagus spears drizzled with orange vinaigrette.*

Chicken Salad:

5 cups cubed cooked chicken

2 scallions, chopped (white &
    tender green parts)

½ cup green or red seedless
    grapes

⅓ cup minced fresh parsley

¼ cup minced fresh basil

¼ cup toasted sliced almonds

⅔ cup mayonnaise

2 tablespoons tarragon vinegar

2 teaspoons Dijon-style mustard

Salt & black pepper

Lettuce leaves (optional)

Radicchio leaves (optional)

Herbed Waffles:

1¾ cups all-purpose flour

½ cup minced fresh parsley

¼ cup grated Parmesan cheese

2 scallions, chopped (white &
    tender green parts)

2 tablespoons minced fresh basil

2 tablespoons minced fresh
    rosemary

1 tablespoon sugar (optional)

1¾ teaspoons baking powder

½ teaspoon baking soda

¼ teaspoon salt

1⅓ cups milk

2 large eggs, at room
    temperature

3 tablespoons butter, melted

2 teaspoons Dijon-style mustard

Prepare the salad: In a medium-size bowl, combine the chicken, scallions, grapes, parsley, basil, and almonds. In a small bowl, whisk together the mayonnaise, vinegar, and mustard until well blended. Add this mixture to the chicken mixture, tossing to coat. Season to taste with salt and pepper. Cover with plastic wrap and set aside at room temperature while preparing waffles.

Prepare the waffles: Preheat the oven to 200°F. Preheat a waffle iron. In a medium-size bowl, combine the flour, parsley, cheese, scallions, basil, rosemary, sugar if desired, baking powder, baking soda, and salt.

In another medium-size bowl, whisk together the milk, eggs, butter, and mustard. Pour this mixture into the dry ingredients, stirring to form a smooth batter.

Lightly grease or spray the grids of the waffle iron. Follow the manufacturer's instructions, or spoon about ⅓ cup batter (amount varies with size of iron) onto the hot iron and spread it almost to the corners of the grids. Close the lid and bake for 2 to 3 minutes, or until the waffles are golden brown, their edges look dry, and they do not stick to the grids. Transfer the baked waffles to the oven, placing them directly on the rack so they will stay crisp. Repeat with the remaining batter.

Arrange the waffles and lettuce leaves on individual serving plates. Spoon the chicken salad over the lettuce. **Makes 9 waffles.**

Curried Corn Waffles with Spicy Ratatouille

Curry powder adds a golden-orange color to these savory waffles. Topped with chunky ratatouille, they make a great lunch or Sunday supper. Use a Belgian waffle iron so the large deep grids can hold the topping. Leftover waffles can be frozen and reheated in a toaster or conventional oven, then served with slices of sharp Cheddar cheese for an interesting sandwich.

Spicy Ratatouille:

½ cup olive oil

1 medium eggplant, cut into 1-inch cubes

1 medium onion, coarsely chopped

3 garlic cloves, minced

1 medium green bell pepper, seeded & cut into ¾-inch pieces

1 medium red bell pepper, seeded & cut into ¾-inch pieces

2 cups canned stewed or crushed tomatoes

1 medium zucchini, cut into ¾-inch pieces

1 tablespoon minced fresh thyme

½ cup fresh minced parsley

1 teaspoon hot-pepper flakes (optional)

Curried Corn Waffles:

1¼ cups yellow cornmeal

1 cup all-purpose flour

1 tablespoon curry powder

1 teaspoon baking powder

1 teaspoon sugar

½ teaspoon baking soda

1¼ cups milk

2 large eggs, at room temperature

3 tablespoons butter, melted

Prepare the ratatouille: In a large heavy skillet, heat the oil over medium heat. Add the eggplant and cook, stirring frequently, for 2 to 3 minutes, or until the edges begin to soften. Add the onion and garlic, and cook, stirring frequently, for 1 to 2 minutes. Add the bell peppers and cook, stirring frequently, for 2 to 3 minutes. Stir in the tomatoes and bring the mixture to a boil. Add the zucchini and thyme. Reduce the heat to low and cook, partially covered, for about 15 to 20 minutes, or until the vegetables are tender but not mushy. Stir in the parsley and hot-pepper flakes and cook for 1 minute more. Remove the pan from the heat.

Prepare the waffles: Preheat the oven to 200°F. Preheat a Belgian waffle iron. In a medium-size bowl, combine the cornmeal, flour, curry powder, baking powder, sugar, and baking soda.

In a small bowl, whisk together the milk, eggs, and butter. Pour this mixture into the dry ingredients, stirring to form a smooth batter.

Lightly grease or spray the grids of the waffle iron. Follow the manufacturer's instructions, or spoon about ⅓ cup batter (amount varies with size of iron) onto the hot iron and spread it almost to the corners of the grids. Close the lid and bake for 1 to 2 minutes, or until the waffles are golden brown, the edges look dry, and they do not stick to the grids. Transfer the baked waffles to the oven, placing them directly on the rack so they will stay crisp. Repeat with the remaining batter.

Transfer the waffles to warmed serving plates and top each serving with the ratatouille. **Makes 8 to 10 waffles.**

Blueberry Buttermilk Pancakes

This is a versatile pancake, lending itself to many variations. The addition of buttermilk, which is low in fat because it is made from skimmed or partly skimmed milk, adds a slightly tangy flavor and an extra-tender texture.

1⅓ cups all-purpose flour

¼ cup whole-wheat flour

1 tablespoon sugar

¾ teaspoon baking powder

¾ teaspoon baking soda

1½ cups buttermilk

2 large eggs, at room temperature

3 tablespoons butter, melted

2 cups fresh or frozen blueberries

Butter & maple syrup or honey, for topping

Preheat the oven to 200°F. In a medium-size bowl, combine both flours, the sugar, baking powder, and baking soda.

In a small bowl, whisk together the buttermilk, eggs, and butter. Pour this mixture into the dry ingredients, stirring to form a smooth batter. Fold in the blueberries.

Heat a griddle or large heavy skillet over medium-high heat until hot, or until a few drops of water sizzle on the surface. Lightly grease the griddle.

Stir the batter. For each pancake, pour about ¼ cup batter onto the hot griddle. Cook for about 2 minutes, or until many bubbles appear on the surface and the edges look dry. Before turning the pancakes, lift the edges to check that the undersides are golden brown. Turn the pancakes and cook for 1 to 2 minutes more, or until the undersides are golden brown. Transfer the pancakes to a baking sheet, cover loosely with foil, and keep warm in the oven. Repeat with the remaining batter.

Transfer the pancakes to warmed serving plates and top each serving with butter and syrup. **Makes 10 to 12 pancakes.**

Raspberry Buttermilk Pancakes: Prepare the batter according to the recipe, but fold in 2 cups fresh, or frozen, raspberries instead of blueberries. Cook as directed.

Banana Buttermilk Pancakes: Prepare the batter according to the recipe, but fold in 2 cups thinly sliced bananas instead of blueberries. Cook as directed.

49

Buckwheat-Molasses Pancakes

This pancake is reminiscent of days past when batters were made with yeast and left on the back of the stove to rise overnight. This batter can be made the night before and left to rise slowly in the refrigerator until morning. Buckwheat flour, made from the seeds of the buckwheat plant, has a distinctively dark color and is rich in minerals and vitamins.

¼ cup warm water

2 teaspoons active dry yeast

1 ⅓ cups all-purpose flour

⅔ cup buckwheat flour

1 tablespoon dark brown sugar

1 ½ teaspoons ground coriander

1 teaspoon cinnamon

1 teaspoon ground ginger

⅛ teaspoon ground cloves

1 ¼ cups milk

2 large eggs, at room temperature

¼ cup molasses

2 tablespoons vegetable oil

Butter & maple syrup or honey, for topping

In a small bowl, combine the water and yeast. Let stand for 5 to 10 minutes, or until the mixture begins to foam. In a medium-size bowl, combine both flours, the brown sugar, coriander, cinnamon, ginger, and cloves.

In another small bowl, whisk together the milk, eggs, molasses, and oil. Stir in the yeast mixture. Pour this mixture into the dry ingredients, stirring to form a smooth batter. Cover the batter with a damp towel and let rise in a warm place for about 1 hour, or until doubled in bulk.

Preheat the oven to 200°F. Heat a griddle or large heavy skillet over medium-high heat until hot, or until a few drops of water sizzle on the surface. Lightly grease the griddle.

Stir the batter. For each pancake, pour about ¼ cup batter onto the hot griddle. Cook for about 2 minutes, or

until many bubbles appear on the surface and the edges look dry. Before turning the pancakes, lift the edges to check that the undersides are golden brown. Turn the pancakes and cook for 1 to 2 minutes more, or until the undersides are golden brown. Transfer the pancakes to a baking sheet, cover loosely with foil, and keep warm in the oven. Repeat with the remaining batter.

Transfer the pancakes to warmed serving plates and top each serving with butter and syrup. **Makes 10 to 12 pancakes.**

Anadama Pancakes with Mixed Oranges

Anadama refers to a combination of cornmeal, rye flour, and molasses that was used frequently in Colonial times, especially for making bread. These sweet and savory flavors work wonderfully in pancakes as well. Mandarin, navel, and blood oranges are used here for the tangy orange topping, although any combination of orange or tangerine varieties can be used.

Mixed Oranges:

2 large navel oranges

2 mandarin oranges, peeled & sliced

2 blood oranges, peeled & sliced

½ cup fresh orange juice

½ teaspoon aniseed (optional)

Anadama Pancakes:

1¼ cups all-purpose flour

⅔ cup rye flour

⅔ cup yellow cornmeal

2 teaspoons baking powder

1 teaspoon baking soda

¼ teaspoon salt

1½ cups milk

2 large eggs, at room temperature

¼ cup packed light brown sugar

¼ cup molasses

3 tablespoons butter, melted

2 teaspoons grated orange zest

Butter & maple syrup, for topping (optional)

Prepare the oranges: Using a sharp knife, cut the peel and all the white pith off the navel oranges. Cut the oranges into segments. In a medium-size nonreactive bowl, combine the navel orange segments, sliced oranges, and orange juice. Sprinkle with the aniseed, if desired. Cover with plastic wrap and chill until ready to use.

Prepare the pancakes: Preheat the oven to 200°F. In a medium-size bowl, combine both flours, the cornmeal,

baking powder, baking soda, and salt.

In another medium-size bowl, whisk together the milk, eggs, brown sugar, molasses, butter, and orange zest. Pour this mixture into the dry ingredients, stirring to form a smooth batter.

Heat a griddle or large heavy skillet over medium-high heat until hot, or until a few drops of water sizzle on the surface. Lightly grease the griddle.

For each pancake, pour about ¼ cup batter onto the hot griddle. Cook for about 2 minutes, or until many bubbles appear on the surface and the edges look dry. Before turning the pancakes, lift the edges to check that the undersides are golden brown. Turn the pancakes and cook for 1 to 2 minutes more, or until the undersides are golden brown. Transfer the pancakes to a baking sheet, cover loosely with foil, and keep warm in the oven. Repeat with the remaining batter.

Transfer the pancakes to warmed serving plates and top each serving with butter and syrup, if desired. Serve the oranges on the side or use as a topping. **Makes 10 to 12 pancakes.**

German Apple Pancake

Here is an easy recipe using basic ingredients that produces stunning results every time. The thin batter, similar to popover batter, is poured over sautéed apples. While it bakes it creates steam, resulting in a puffy pancake, golden and crisp on the outside, soft and eggy on the inside. Sliced fresh pears or peaches can be used instead of apples; a handful of fresh blackberries or toasted nuts can be added to the fruit for an interesting variation.

1 cup milk

3 large eggs, at room
temperature

¾ cup all-purpose flour

3 tablespoons granulated sugar

2 tablespoons butter

2 medium cooking apples such
as Granny Smith, peeled,
cored & cut into ¼-inch slices

¼ teaspoon cinnamon

Confectioners' sugar, for dusting

Lemon wedges (optional)

Preheat the oven to 375°F. In a medium-size bowl, whisk together the milk, eggs, flour, and 2 tablespoons granulated sugar.

In a large heavy ovenproof skillet over medium-high heat, melt the butter. Add the apples, cinnamon, and the remaining 1 tablespoon granulated sugar. Reduce the heat to medium and cook, stirring occasionally, for 2 to 3 minutes, or until the apples are softened

slightly. Remove the pan from the heat. Pour the batter over the apples in the pan. Place the pan in the oven and bake for 30 to 35 minutes, or until the pancake is lightly browned and puffy.

Remove the pan from the oven and cut the pancake into wedges. Transfer the wedges to warmed serving plates, dust with confectioners' sugar, and serve with lemon wedges, if desired. **Serves 6 to 8**

Sourdough Pancakes with Sorghum Syrup

The mild molasses flavor of sorghum syrup stands up well to the sour taste of these light pancakes. Although the sourdough starter takes several days to fully establish itself, it can be used after about 8 hours, but the sour taste will not be as intense. If you can, plan ahead so the starter can ripen for 3 to 5 days.

1 ⅓ cups all-purpose flour
¼ cup whole-wheat flour
¾ teaspoon baking powder
¼ teaspoon salt
1 cup milk
¾ cup sourdough starter
(see facing page)

2 large eggs, at room
temperature
3 tablespoons butter, melted
1 tablespoon honey
Butter & sorghum syrup,
for topping

Preheat the oven to 200°F. In a medium-size bowl, combine both flours, the baking powder, and salt.

In another medium-size bowl, whisk together the milk, sourdough starter, eggs, butter, and honey. Pour this mixture into the dry ingredients, stirring quickly to form a smooth batter.

Heat a griddle or large heavy skillet over medium-high heat until hot, or until a few drops of water sizzle on the surface. Lightly grease the griddle.

For each pancake, pour about ¼ cup batter onto the hot griddle. Cook for about 1½ to 2 minutes, or until many bubbles appear on the surface and the edges look dry. Before turning the pancakes, lift the edges to check that the undersides are golden brown. Turn the pancakes and cook for 30 to 45 seconds more, or until the undersides are golden brown. Transfer the pancakes to a baking sheet, cover loosely with foil, and keep warm in the oven. Repeat with the remaining batter.

Transfer the pancakes to warmed serving plates and top each serving with butter and warm sorghum syrup. **Makes 10 to 12 pancakes.**

To make sourdough starter: In a medium-size nonreactive bowl, combine 2 cups warm water, 1 tablespoon dry active yeast, and 2 tablespoons honey. Let stand for about 10 minutes, or until it becomes foamy. Using a wooden spoon, stir in 1 cup all-purpose flour and 1 cup whole-wheat flour until smooth. Transfer the mixture to a nonreactive container, large enough to allow the starter to double in bulk. Cover and let stand in a warm place for 3 to 5 days, stirring the mixture at least three times daily. It will rise and fall, remain bubbly, and have a pleasant sour smell. When the starter develops a flavor and aroma that are pleasing to you, it is ready to use. The starter will keep indefinitely if stored, tightly covered, in the refrigerator. If it develops an orange or pink color, discard it.

Once a starter is made, it must be replenished at least once every 2 to 3 weeks to keep it alive. To replenish, remove 1 cup starter and discard it. Add 1 cup flour and 1 cup tepid water to the remaining starter, stirring until smooth. Cover and let stand in a warm place for 8 to 10 hours before refrigerating it again.

Oat Cakes with Cran-Raspberry Topping & Crème Fraîche

Whole oats make these pancakes thick and chewy. The cran-raspberry topping can be made up to 2 days ahead, but the oat cakes should be prepared just before serving. You can make your own crème fraîche by stirring 1 tablespoon of buttermilk into 1 cup of heavy cream and leaving it, covered, in a warm place for 24 to 36 hours (refrigerate it 4 to 6 hours before serving).

Cran-Raspberry Topping:

1 (12-ounce) bag fresh or frozen cranberries

¾ cup orange juice

½ cup sugar

2½ cups fresh raspberries, or 1 (12-ounce) bag unsweetened frozen raspberries

Oat Cakes:

1 cup rolled oats

¾ cup quick-cooking oats

½ cup all-purpose flour

¼ cup whole-wheat flour

1 teaspoon baking powder

½ teaspoon baking soda

¼ teaspoon salt

1 cup milk

2 large eggs, at room temperature

3 tablespoons butter, melted

3 tablespoons honey

Crème fraîche, for topping

Cinnamon or freshly grated nutmeg, for dusting (optional)

Prepare the topping: In a medium-size saucepan, combine the cranberries, orange juice, and sugar. Bring the mixture to a boil over medium-high heat. Reduce the heat to medium-low, cover, and cook, stirring occasionally, for about 8 to 10 minutes, or until most of the cranberries have popped. Remove the pan from the heat and stir in the raspberries. Serve warm or chilled.

Prepare the oat cakes: Preheat the oven to 200°F. In a medium-size bowl, combine both oats, both flours, the baking powder, baking soda, and salt.

In a small bowl, whisk together the milk, eggs, butter, and honey. Pour this mixture into the dry ingredients, stirring to form an almost smooth batter.

Heat a griddle or large heavy skillet over medium-high heat until hot, or until a few drops of water sizzle on the surface. Lightly grease the griddle.

For each pancake, pour about ⅓ cup batter onto the hot griddle. Cook for about 2 minutes, or until many bubbles appear on the surface and the edges look dry. Before turning the pancakes, lift the edges to check that the undersides are golden brown. Turn the pancakes and cook for 1 to 2 minutes more, or until the undersides are golden brown. Transfer the pancakes to a baking sheet, cover loosely with foil, and keep warm in the oven. Repeat with the remaining batter.

Transfer the pancakes to a warmed serving platter. Dust with cinnamon, if desired. Serve with crème fraîche and cran-raspberry topping. **Makes 9 thick pancakes.**

Hazelnut-Honey Pancakes with Raspberries

picture p. 2

The batter for these elegant pancakes uses both finely and coarsely chopped hazelnuts, adding a rich, nutty taste and a crunchy texture. Toasting the nuts intensifies their full flavor and nicely complements the tart fresh raspberries. Serve this dish for a special-occasion breakfast or brunch.

1½ cups shelled hazelnuts
1⅓ cups all-purpose flour
¾ teaspoon baking powder
½ teaspoon baking soda
⅔ cup half-and-half
⅔ cup milk

3 large eggs, at room temperature
3 tablespoons butter, melted
2 tablespoons honey
1½ teaspoons pure vanilla extract
Butter & sugar, for topping
Fresh raspberries, for topping

Preheat the oven to 350°F. Spread the hazelnuts on an ungreased baking sheet and toast for 15 minutes. Transfer the nuts to a towel. Fold the towel over the nuts and rub vigorously to remove the skins. Transfer the nuts to a cutting board. Coarsely chop half the nuts and finely chop the remaining half. Set aside to cool.

In a medium-size bowl, combine all the chopped hazelnuts, flour, baking powder, and baking soda.

In another medium-size bowl, whisk together the half-and-half, milk, eggs, butter, honey, and vanilla. Pour this mixture into the dry ingredients, stirring to form a smooth batter.

Reduce the oven temperature to 200°F. Heat a griddle or large heavy skillet over medium-high heat until hot,

60

Fresh-picked raspberries

or until a few drops of water sizzle on the surface. Lightly grease the griddle.

For each pancake, pour about ¼ cup batter onto the hot griddle. Cook for about 2 minutes, or until the bubbles that form begin to pop and the edges look dry. Before turning the pancakes, lift the edges to check that the undersides are golden brown. Turn the pancakes and cook for 1 to 2 minutes more, or until the undersides are golden brown. Transfer the pancakes to a baking sheet, cover loosely with foil, and keep warm in the oven. Repeat with the remaining batter.

Transfer the pancakes to warmed serving plates and top each serving with butter and sugar, then the fresh raspberries. **Makes 10 to 12 pancakes.**

Panettone Christmas Pancakes with Pistachio Butter

Panettone is an Italian sweet yeast bread studded with candied fruit, citron, and sometimes nuts. Here, this traditional Christmas bread takes the form of rich sweet pancakes filled with your choice of dried fruit. Dried pears, peaches, pineapple, apricots, apples, or dates can be used in any combination. Candied citron is made from a thick-skinned type of lemon grown chiefly for its skin. It is available in most large supermarkets.

Pistachio Butter:

½ cup (1 stick) unsalted butter, softened

2 tablespoons finely chopped pistachios

Panettone Pancakes:

2 cups all-purpose flour

½ cup sugar

½ cup mixed dried fruit, finely chopped

1 tablespoon candied citron, candied lemon peel, or candied orange peel

1¾ teaspoons baking powder

½ teaspoon baking soda

¼ teaspoon freshly grated nutmeg

1¼ cups half-and-half

3 large eggs, at room temperature

3 tablespoons butter, melted

Maple syrup, for topping

Fresh raspberries, for topping (optional)

Prepare the butter: In a food processor fitted with the metal blade, combine the butter and pistachios and process for 5 seconds. Scrape down the sides of the bowl and process for 3 to 5 seconds more, or until well blended. Scrape the butter into a small bowl, cover with plastic wrap, and chill until ready to serve.

Prepare the pancakes: Preheat the oven to 200°F. In a medium-size bowl,

combine the flour, sugar, dried fruit, citron, baking powder, baking soda, and nutmeg.

In another medium-size bowl, whisk together the half-and-half, eggs, and butter. Pour this mixture into the dry ingredients, stirring to form a smooth batter.

Heat a griddle or large heavy skillet over medium-high heat until hot, or until a few drops of water sizzle on the surface. Lightly grease the griddle.

For each pancake, pour about ¼ cup batter onto the hot griddle. Cook for about 1½ to 2 minutes, or until many bubbles appear on the surface and the edges look dry. Before turning the pancakes, lift the edges to check that the undersides are golden brown. Turn the pancakes and cook for 1 minute more, or until the undersides are golden brown. Transfer the pancakes to a baking sheet, cover loosely with foil, and keep warm in the oven. Repeat with the remaining batter.

Transfer the pancakes to warmed serving plates and top each serving with pistachio butter and syrup. Serve with raspberries, if desired. **Makes 10 to 12 pancakes.**

Blue Corn Pancakes with Honey-Red Chile Butter

*In New Mexico, blue corn, with its distinctive color and earthy flavor,
is roasted and made into a porridge called* atole, *traditionally served with red
chile sauce. The flavors are recreated in this pancake and topping, and are
sweetened with honey. Pine nuts, called* piñon *in New Mexico, come from several
varieties of pine trees and have a light, delicate flavor.*

Honey–Red Chile Butter:

½ cup (1 stick) unsalted butter, softened

1 tablespoon ground mild New Mexican red chile

2 tablespoons honey

Blue Corn Pancakes:

¼ cup pine nuts

1¼ cups blue cornmeal

¾ cup all-purpose flour

¾ teaspoon baking powder

¾ teaspoon baking soda

1 cup milk

2 large eggs, at room temperature

2 tablespoons butter, melted

2 tablespoons honey

Honey, for topping

Prepare the butter: In a food processor fitted with the metal blade, combine the butter, red chile, and honey; process until smooth and well blended. Scrape the butter into a small bowl, cover with plastic wrap, and chill until ready to serve.

Prepare the pancakes: Preheat the oven to 200°F. In a small skillet over medium heat, toast the pine nuts, stirring frequently, for 2 to 3 minutes, or until fragrant and golden. Remove the pan from the heat and let cool slightly.

In a medium-size bowl, combine the pine nuts, cornmeal, flour, baking powder, and baking soda. In a small bowl, whisk together the milk, eggs,

butter, and honey. Pour this mixture into the dry ingredients, stirring to form a smooth batter.

Heat a griddle or large heavy skillet over medium-high heat until hot, or until a few drops of water sizzle on the surface. Lightly grease the griddle.

For each pancake, pour about ¼ cup batter onto the hot griddle. Cook for about 2 minutes, or until many bubbles appear on the surface and the edges look dry. Before turning the pancakes, lift the edges to check that the undersides are golden brown. Turn the pancakes and cook for 1 to 2 minutes more, or until the undersides are golden brown. Transfer the pancakes to a baking sheet, cover loosely with foil, and keep warm in the oven. Repeat with the remaining batter.

Transfer the pancakes to warmed serving plates and top each serving with the honey–red chile butter and additional honey. **Makes 10 to 12 pancakes.**

Dutch Babie

*A close relative of the popover and Yorkshire pudding, the Dutch Babie
rises and falls as it bakes so the center stays soft and eggy. It's traditionally served
with a sprinkling of confectioners' sugar and a squeeze of fresh lemon juice.
The crater-like shape makes it perfect for filling with fresh or cooked fruit.*

1 tablespoon butter

1 cup all-purpose flour

1 tablespoon granulated sugar

1 ¼ cups milk

2 large eggs, at room
temperature

¼ teaspoon salt

Confectioners' sugar, for dusting

Sliced fresh nectarines and
blackberries, for topping

Preheat the oven to 375°F. Put the butter in a 9-inch pie pan and place it in the oven to melt. Meanwhile, in a large bowl, combine the flour, granulated sugar, milk, eggs, and salt. Using an electric mixer set at medium-high, beat the mixture for 1½ to 2 minutes, or until smooth. Remove the pan from the oven and carefully swirl to evenly coat the bottom with the butter. Pour the batter into the pan and bake for about 30 minutes, or until the edges have risen and are crisp and golden brown, and the center is set but still soft.

Remove the pan from the oven and dust with confectioners' sugar. Cut the pancake into wedges, top with nectarines and blackberries, and serve immediately. **Serves 6 to 8.**

Basic Crêpes

There are many versions of crêpes, but the goal is always the same: thin, tender, lightly browned pancakes. They provide an interesting envelope for all sorts of sweet and savory fillings. As with most pancakes, the second side never browns as nicely as the first, so you generally want to roll the crêpes with the first side facing out.

1 cup all-purpose flour

¾ cup milk

¾ cup water

3 large eggs, at room temperature

2 tablespoons butter, melted & cooled

½ teaspoon salt

In a food processor fitted with the metal blade, combine all of the ingredients and process for 10 to 15 seconds, or until smooth. Scrape down the sides of the bowl and process for 5 to 10 seconds more. Transfer the batter to a medium-size bowl, cover with plastic wrap, and chill for 1 hour.

Heat a 6-inch crêpe pan or small skillet over medium-high heat until hot, or until a few drops of water sizzle on the surface. Lightly grease the pan. Pour about 3 tablespoons batter into the pan, tilting to coat the bottom evenly. Cook for about 1 minute, or until the edges look lacy and begin to pull away from the pan. Before turning the crêpe, lift the edges to check that the underside is lightly browned. Turn the crêpe and cook for 15 to 30 seconds, or until the underside is lightly browned. Transfer the crêpe to a sheet of waxed paper. Repeat with the remaining batter, greasing the pan as necessary. **Makes 14 crêpes.**

NOTE: Crêpes can be made ahead. Stack completely cooled crêpes, wrap with foil, and refrigerate up to 5 days or freeze up to 2 months. Thaw at room temperature.

Crêpe-making, France

Crêpes with Butter and Sugar: Prepare the crêpes according to the recipe. As soon as each crêpe is finished, brush one side with 1 teaspoon melted butter and sprinkle with ¾ teaspoon sugar. Fold the crêpe into quarters and transfer it to a warmed serving platter. Sprinkle the filled crêpes with additional sugar and serve immediately. Decorate with sprigs of fresh mint, if desired.

Chocolate Crêpes: In a food processor fitted with the metal blade, combine ¾ cup all-purpose flour, ¾ cup milk, ¾ cup water, 6 tablespoons unsweetened nonalkalized cocoa powder, 3 large eggs, ¼ cup sugar, 3 tablespoons melted unsalted butter, 1 teaspoon pure vanilla extract, and ¼ teaspoon salt. Process for 10 to 15 seconds, or until well blended. Scrape down the sides of the bowl and process again for 5 to 10 seconds. Transfer the mixture to a medium-size bowl, cover with plastic wrap, and chill for 1 hour. Cook as directed. **Makes 12 crêpes.**

Cheese Blintzes

Blintzes are simply filled and folded crêpes sautéed in butter.
Cheese blintzes are the most traditional, often topped
with applesauce and sour cream. Though dessertlike in nature, blintzes
can be a breakfast, brunch, or main dish as well.

1 recipe Basic Crêpes (p. 68)

Cheese Filling:

1½ pounds farmer cheese

2 large eggs, at room
    temperature

2 tablespoons confectioners'
    sugar

1 teaspoon grated lemon zest

½ teaspoon pure vanilla extract

¼ teaspoon cinnamon

4 to 6 tablespoons butter

Fresh berries, sour cream &
    lemon zest, for topping

Prepare the crêpes according to the recipe. Set aside. Preheat the oven to 350°F.

Prepare the filling: In a large bowl, combine all of the filling ingredients, stirring until smooth and well blended.

Place 1 crêpe on a work surface. Spoon 3 tablespoons of the filling down the center. Fold the long edges of the crêpe over the filling. Turn the crêpe seam side down and tuck under the shorter open ends. Repeat filling and folding the remaining crêpes.

In a large skillet over medium heat, melt 2 tablespoons butter. Cook the blintzes in batches, seam side down, for about 2 minutes, or until the undersides are lightly browned. Turn the blintzes and cook for 1 minute more or until the undersides are lightly browned. Transfer the blintzes to a baking sheet and keep warm in the oven. Repeat cooking the remaining blintzes, adding more butter as needed.

When all the blintzes are cooked, transfer them to warmed serving plates

and top each serving with berries, sour cream, and lemon zest. **Makes 14 blintzes.**

Blueberry Blintzes: In a medium-size saucepan, combine 3 cups fresh or frozen blueberries, 1 cup blueberry preserves, 2 teaspoons fresh lemon juice, and ¼ teaspoon cinnamon. Cook over medium heat, stirring frequently, for 3 to 5 minutes, or until the mixture is heated through. Fill, fold, cook, and serve as directed.

Chocolate Crêpes with Chocolate Chip Ricotta Filling

These bittersweet chocolate crêpes are wrapped around a whipped cream and ricotta cheese filling, studded with mini chocolate chips for a bit of crunch. Served in a pool of tart raspberry sauce, they make an elegant and memorable dessert.

1 recipe Chocolate Crêpes (p. 69)

Chocolate Chip Ricotta Filling:

¾ cup heavy cream

2 tablespoons granulated sugar

1 cup ricotta cheese, low-fat milk, or whole milk

1 tablespoon almond-flavored liqueur (Amaretto, optional)

4 ounces (⅔ cup) semisweet mini chocolate chips

Raspberry Coulis:

1 (12-ounce) bag unsweetened frozen raspberries, thawed

2 tablespoons confectioners' sugar

2 teaspoons fresh lemon juice

Prepare the crêpes according to the recipe and set aside.

Prepare the filling: In a medium-size bowl, using an electric mixer set at high, beat the cream and granulated sugar until soft peaks form. Reduce the mixer speed to medium and beat in the ricotta cheese and liqueur, if desired. Beat until the mixture is stiff, about 45 seconds. Using a rubber spatula, gently and thoroughly fold in the chocolate chips. Cover with plastic wrap and chill until ready to use.

Prepare the coulis: In a food processor fitted with the metal blade, combine the raspberries, confectioners' sugar, and lemon juice, and process until pureed. Strain the mixture through a medium-fine sieve set over a small bowl; discard the seeds.

To assemble the crêpes: Place 1 crêpe on a work surface and spoon ¼ cup of the

filling down the center. Fold the crêpe in half over the filling, then fold the crêpe in half again to form a triangle. Place the folded crêpe on a serving platter. Fill and fold the remaining crêpes. Serve with raspberry coulis. **Makes 12 crêpes.**

Flambéed Dessert Crêpes with Apricot Preserves

Reminiscent of Crêpes Suzette, these dessert crêpes are spread with apricot preserves, folded in quarters, sprinkled with sugar, and flambéed with a mixture of warm Cognac and orange-flavored liqueur. The flaming presentation is dramatic, especially in a darkened room. Remember to avert your face when igniting the barely warm liquor (overheated liquor will not ignite).

1 recipe Basic Crêpes (p. 68)
1 cup apricot preserves
¼ cup orange-flavored liqueur (Cointreau)

¼ cup Cognac or brandy
1 to 2 tablespoons sugar

Prepare the crêpes according to the recipe. Preheat the oven to 350°F.

Place 1 crêpe on a work surface and spread about 1 tablespoon apricot preserves over it. Fold in half, then in quarters, and place in a shallow baking dish or heatproof platter with a rimmed edge. Repeat filling and folding the remaining crêpes, arranging them in the dish.

Bake the filled crêpes for 12 to 15 minutes, or until heated through. Meanwhile, in a small saucepan, combine the liqueur and Cognac. Heat over low heat, stirring occasionally, until warm.

Remove the baking dish from the oven and sprinkle the crêpes with the sugar. Light the liqueur mixture using a long fireplace match and carefully pour the flaming liquid over the crêpes. Serve the crêpes when the flames have died out. **Makes 14 crêpes.**

Barley, Blue Corn & Buckwheat Pancakes

Blue cornmeal, ground from a field corn variety with blue kernels, lends a bluish-gray color to these nutritious, nutty-flavored pancakes, light on fat but not on flavor.

⅔ cup barley flour

⅔ cup blue cornmeal

⅔ cup buckwheat flour

1 teaspoon baking powder

½ teaspoon baking soda

1½ cups buttermilk

2 large eggs, at room temperature

2 tablespoons vegetable oil

1 tablespoon honey

Maple syrup, for topping

Preheat the oven to 200°F. In a medium-size bowl, combine the barley flour, cornmeal, buckwheat flour, baking powder, and baking soda.

In a small bowl, whisk together the buttermilk, eggs, oil, and honey. Pour this mixture into the dry ingredients, stirring to form a smooth batter.

Heat a griddle or large heavy skillet over medium-high heat until hot, or until a few drops of water sizzle on the surface. Lightly grease the griddle.

Stir the batter. For each pancake, pour about ¼ cup batter onto the hot griddle. Cook for about 2 minutes, or until many bubbles appear on the surface and the edges look dry. Before turning the pancakes, lift the edges to check that the undersides are golden brown. Turn the pancakes and cook for 1 to 2 minutes more, or until the undersides are golden brown. Transfer the pancakes to a baking sheet, cover loosely with foil, and keep warm in the oven. Repeat with the remaining batter.

Transfer the pancakes to warmed serving plates and top each serving with syrup. **Makes 10 to 12 pancakes.**

Blini

For years these yeast-raised pancakes have been a traditional part of a Russian pre-Lenten celebration called Maslenitsa (meaning "butter festival"), where stacks of them are served alongside bowls of melted butter and sour cream ~ and plenty of vodka. They have also been paired with pickled herring, smoked sturgeon, every type of caviar, finely chopped mushroom and onion mixtures, and even homemade preserves. Here, the blini are made in appetizer portions and served with a creamy smoked trout topping.

Smoked Trout Spread:

- 1 (8-ounce) package cream cheese, softened
- 4 to 5 ounces smoked trout, skin and bones removed
- 3 tablespoons sour cream
- 1 tablespoon fresh lemon juice
- Salt & black pepper
- 2 teaspoons minced fresh dill (optional)
- 2 teaspoons prepared horseradish (optional)

Blini:

- ⅓ cup warm water
- 2 teaspoons active dry yeast
- ¾ cup all-purpose flour
- 1 teaspoon sugar
- 2 large eggs, separated, at room temperature
- ¼ teaspoon salt
- ½ cup milk
- 3 tablespoons butter, melted

Sprigs fresh dill, for decoration (optional)

Prepare the spread: In a medium-size bowl, using an electric mixer set at medium, beat the cream cheese until smooth and creamy; scrape down the sides of the bowl. Add the smoked trout and beat until just blended. Beat in the sour cream, lemon juice, and salt and pepper to taste. Beat in the dill and horseradish if desired. Scrape the mixture into a small bowl, cover with plastic wrap,

and set aside while you prepare the blini.

Prepare the blini: In a small bowl, combine the water and yeast. Let stand for 5 to 10 minutes, or until the mixture begins to foam. In a medium-size bowl, combine the flour, sugar, egg yolks, salt, milk, butter, and yeast mixture, stirring to form a smooth batter. Cover the batter with a damp towel and let rise in a warm place for about 1½ hours, or until doubled in bulk.

In a small bowl, using an electric mixer set at high, beat the egg whites until stiff peaks form. Using a rubber spatula, gently and thoroughly fold the egg whites into the risen batter.

Heat a griddle or large heavy skillet over medium-high heat until hot, or until a few drops of water sizzle on the surface. Lightly grease the griddle.

For each pancake, pour about 2 tablespoons batter onto the griddle. Cook over medium heat for about 30 to 45 seconds, or until many bubbles appear on the surface. Before turning the blini, lift the edges to check that the undersides are golden brown. Turn the pancakes and cook for 20 to 30 seconds more, or until the undersides are golden brown. Transfer the blini to a baking sheet, cover loosely with foil, and keep warm in the oven. Repeat with the remaining batter.

Transfer the blini to a serving platter and top each one with a spoonful of the trout spread and decorate with dill, if desired. **Makes 24 blini.**

Smoked Salmon Spread: Omit the horseradish and substitute 4 to 5 ounces skinned and boned smoked salmon for the smoked trout. Proceed as directed.

Sweet Corn Cakes

Sweet corn is a uniquely American food, and so no doubt are corn cakes. Bound with egg and bread crumbs, these cakes are sometimes referred to as corn fritters. They are perfect for breakfast with eggs and bacon, or as a side dish with grilled meats or fish. Serve them topped with sour cream, cilantro, and the Roasted Pepper–Tomato Relish given here, or on their own.

Roasted Pepper–Tomato Relish:

1 medium red bell pepper

4 ripe medium plum tomatoes such as Roma, cut in half lengthwise

½ onion, cut into 4 large pieces

2 garlic cloves, minced

2 tablespoons olive oil

½ teaspoon ground cumin

Salt & black pepper

2 tablespoons balsamic or red wine vinegar

Sweet Corn Cakes:

2½ cups fresh or frozen corn kernels, thawed if frozen

1½ cups fresh bread crumbs

⅓ cup all-purpose flour

¼ cup grated Parmesan cheese

3 large eggs, at room temperature

½ cup finely chopped red bell pepper

2 scallions, chopped (white & tender green parts)

¼ cup minced fresh parsley

Salt & black pepper

Sour cream, for topping (optional)

Minced fresh cilantro, for topping (optional)

Prepare the relish: Preheat the broiler. Place the bell pepper under the broiler 4 inches from the heat source. Broil, turning frequently with a fork, for 15 minutes, or until the skin is charred all over. Transfer the bell pepper to a paper bag, close the bag, and set aside to steam for 10 to 15 minutes. Remove the

cooled bell pepper from the bag. Using a small knife, peel off the charred skin. Remove the core and seeds and cut into thin strips.

Preheat the oven to 450°F. In a shallow baking pan, combine the tomatoes, onion, and garlic. Add the oil, cumin, and salt and pepper to taste; toss to coat. Bake, uncovered, for about 25 minutes, or until the tomatoes and onions are softened but not mushy and are browned on the edges. Remove the pan from the oven and let cool completely.

Transfer the vegetables to a cutting board and coarsely chop them. Transfer to a medium-size bowl. Stir in the roasted bell pepper and vinegar. Cover with plastic wrap and leave at room temperature until ready to serve.

Prepare the corn cakes: Reduce the oven temperature to 200°F. In a medium-size bowl, combine the corn, bread crumbs, flour, cheese, eggs, bell pepper, scallions, and parsley until well blended. Season to taste with salt and pepper.

Heat a griddle or large heavy skillet over medium-high heat until hot, or until a few drops of water sizzle on the surface. Lightly grease the griddle.

For each corn cake, spoon a generous 3 tablespoons batter onto the hot griddle and flatten it slightly to about 4 inches in diameter. Cook for about 2 to 3 minutes, or until the undersides are lightly browned. Turn the corn cakes and cook for 1½ minutes more, or until the undersides are lightly browned. Transfer the corn cakes to a baking sheet or ovenproof platter and keep warm in the oven. Repeat with the remaining batter.

Transfer the corn cakes to warmed serving plates and top each serving with the relish, or serve on the side. Garnish with sour cream and cilantro, if desired. **Makes 12 to 14 corn cakes.**

Potato Pancakes with Roasted Garlic & Goat Cheese

Many cultures have some version of a potato pancake, made with raw, cooked, mashed, or sliced potatoes. This recipe is of the Eastern European tradition, updated with the addition of mild-flavored roasted garlic and fresh crumbled goat cheese. The cakes make a great main course when served with a hearty green salad, or as an accompaniment to grilled lamb, chicken, or fish. By omitting the roasted garlic and goat cheese and serving the pancakes with sour cream and applesauce, you can make a dish similar to the classic Jewish latkes.

3 roasted garlic cloves, mashed

4 medium baking potatoes such as Russet or Idaho, peeled & grated

½ cup finely chopped onion

¼ cup all-purpose flour

4 ounces soft mild goat cheese, crumbled

2 large eggs, at room temperature

3 tablespoons vegetable oil

Preheat the oven to 200°F. In a medium-size bowl, combine the roasted garlic, potatoes, onion, flour, cheese, and eggs until well blended.

In a large heavy skillet, heat the oil over medium-high heat. For each pancake, spoon about ⅓ cup batter into the skillet and flatten it slightly to about 4 inches in diameter. Cook the pancakes for about 2 minutes, or until the undersides are crisp and golden brown.

Turn the pancakes and cook about 1 to 2 minutes, or until the undersides are crisp and golden brown. Remove the pancakes to paper towels to drain, then transfer to a baking sheet or ovenproof platter and keep warm in the oven. Repeat with the remaining batter.

Transfer the pancakes to warmed serving plates. **Makes 8 to 10 pancakes.**

To roast garlic: Preheat the oven to 375°F. Place 1 whole head of garlic in a

Fresh garlic, Provence

small baking dish and drizzle it with 2 teaspoons olive oil. Cover the dish tightly with foil and bake for about 25 minutes, or until the cloves are soft and tender. Remove the pan from the oven, uncover, and let cool. Cut the stem end from the garlic head and scoop out the cloves. To store, wrap the cooled garlic head in plastic and refrigerate for up to 2 weeks.

Fresh Ginger & Carrot Skillet Pancake

Freshly grated ginger adds a slightly peppery bite to this variation of a traditional Finnish recipe. The pancake itself is on the sweet side and has a texture almost like rice pudding, with a crunchy bread crumb topping. Equally delicious right from the oven or at room temperature, this dish belongs at your next brunch buffet.

1 cup milk

½ cup half-and-half

3 large eggs, at room temperature

1 tablespoon light brown sugar

3 cups peeled & grated carrots

½ cup cooked rice

1 tablespoon grated fresh ginger

2 tablespoons butter

⅓ cup dry bread crumbs

Preheat the oven to 350°F. Generously grease a large heavy ovenproof skillet.

In a medium-size bowl, whisk together the milk, half-and-half, eggs, and brown sugar until well blended and smooth. Stir in the carrots, rice, and ginger. Pour the mixture into the prepared skillet.

In a small skillet over medium heat, melt the butter. Add the bread crumbs and cook over medium-high heat, stirring frequently, for about 2 to 3 minutes, or until lightly browned. Sprinkle the bread crumbs evenly over the carrot batter.

Bake for 30 to 35 minutes, or until the pancake is set and a skewer or toothpick inserted into the center comes out clean. Remove the skillet from the oven, cut the pancake into wedges, and serve immediately. **Serves 6 to 8.**

Wild Rice & Smoked Cheddar Pancakes

These hearty, nutty-tasting pancakes accented by smoked Cheddar are a great side dish to serve with leftover Thanksgiving turkey. They can also be made into small pancakes and served as an appetizer topped with a sliver of smoked turkey or chicken and cranberry sauce.

1 cup all-purpose flour

¼ cup minced fresh parsley

2 scallions, chopped (white & tender green parts)

2 teaspoons minced fresh sage leaves or 1 teaspoon dried sage leaves

2 teaspoons baking powder

½ teaspoon salt

¼ teaspoon black pepper

Pinch of cayenne (optional)

1 cup milk

3 large eggs

3 tablespoons butter, melted

1½ cups cooked wild rice

¾ cup shredded smoked Cheddar cheese

Preheat the oven to 200°F. In a medium-size bowl, combine the flour, parsley, scallions, sage, baking powder, salt, pepper, and cayenne, if desired.

In a small bowl, whisk together the milk, eggs, and butter. Pour this mixture into the dry ingredients, stirring with a few quick strokes to form a lumpy batter. Add the rice and cheese, stirring until well blended.

Heat a griddle or large heavy skillet over medium-high heat until hot, or until a few drops of water sizzle on the surface. Lightly grease the griddle.

For each pancake, pour about ¼ cup batter onto the hot griddle. Cook for about 1½ minutes, until many bubbles appear on the surface and the edges look dry. Before turning the pancakes, lift the edges to check that the undersides are

golden brown. Turn the pancakes and cook for 1 minute more, or until the undersides are golden brown. Transfer the pancakes to a baking sheet, cover loosely with foil, and keep warm in the oven. Repeat with the remaining batter.

Transfer the pancakes to warmed serving plates. **Makes 10 to 12 pancakes.**

Irish Soda Pancakes

Currants and caraway seeds add just the right balance of sweet and savory tastes to these simple pancakes. Although you can use low-fat cottage cheese in the recipe, whole-milk cottage cheese will provide a richer flavor and texture. With Canadian bacon and quick-sautéed watercress, they are perfect for a quick and easy light supper or weekend brunch.

Irish Soda Pancakes:

2 cups all-purpose flour

1 1/4 cups milk

1 cup small-curd cottage cheese

2 large eggs, at room temperature

3 tablespoons butter, melted

2 tablespoons sugar

2 teaspoons baking powder

1/2 teaspoon baking soda

1/3 cup dried currants

1 teaspoon caraway seeds

Maple syrup or honey, for topping

Bacon and Watercress:

12 slices Canadian bacon

1 bunch watercress, well rinsed

2 tablespoons apple cider vinegar

Prepare the pancakes: Preheat the oven to 200°F. In a food processor fitted with the metal blade, combine all the pancake ingredients except the currants and caraway seeds. Process for 3 to 5 seconds, or until well blended. Add the currants and caraway seeds and process by pulsing once or twice to incorporate them.

Heat a griddle or large heavy skille over medium-high heat until hot, c until a few drops of water sizzle on th surface. Lightly grease the griddle.

For each pancake pour about 1/4 cu batter onto the hot griddle. Cook fo about 2 minutes, or until many bubble appear on the surface and the edge look dry. Before turning the pancakes, li

the edges to check that the undersides are golden brown. Turn the pancakes and cook for 1 to 2 minutes more, or until the undersides are golden brown. Transfer the pancakes to a baking sheet, cover loosely with foil, and keep warm in the oven. Repeat with the remaining batter.

Prepare the bacon and watercress: Add the bacon slices to the hot griddle and cook for about 1 minute on each side, or until lightly browned. Transfer the bacon to a plate. Add the watercress to the hot griddle and sprinkle with the vinegar. Cook, stirring frequently, until the greens begin to wilt. Remove the pan from the heat.

Transfer the pancakes to serving plates and top each serving with syrup or honey. Serve with the bacon and water-cress. **Serves 4 to 6 (12 to 16 pancakes).**

Spinach & Gruyère Crêpes

Crêpes aux épinard, *or spinach crêpes, is a classic French dish traditionally served with roasted meats. This version uses a tasty spinach and cheese mixture as a filling instead. You can prepare this recipe ahead of time and arrange the filled crêpes in the baking dish, then bake just before serving. These crêpes make a wonderful first course or luncheon entrée.*

1 recipe Basic Crêpes (p. 68)

Béchamel Sauce:

2 cups milk

4 tablespoons (½ stick) butter

3 tablespoons all-purpose flour

¼ teaspoon salt

⅛ teaspoon nutmeg

Spinach Filling:

1 (10-ounce) package frozen chopped spinach, thawed & squeezed dry

1 scallion, chopped (white & tender green parts)

3 tablespoons minced fresh parsley

1½ cups shredded Gruyère cheese

¼ cup grated Parmesan cheese

Salt & black pepper

Grated Parmesan cheese, for sprinkling

Prepare the crêpes according to the recipe and set aside.

Prepare the sauce: In a medium-size saucepan, bring the milk just to a simmer. Remove the pan from the heat. Keep warm.

In a small skillet over medium heat, melt the butter. Add the flour and whisk vigorously to blend and dissolve any lumps. Cook, whisking constantly, for about 1 minute. Add ½ cup warm milk and whisk until smooth. Slowly whisk in an additional ½ cup milk until well blended. Return this mixture to the saucepan with the remaining milk.

Bring the mixture to a boil over medium heat, whisking constantly. Add the

salt and nutmeg and cook, whisking constantly, for 1 minute, or until thickened. Remove the pan from the heat. Keep warm.

Prepare the filling: In a large bowl, combine the spinach, scallion, parsley, Gruyère, Parmesan, and 1½ cups béchamel sauce until well blended. Season to taste with salt and pepper.

To assemble the crêpes: Preheat the oven to 350°F. Place 1 crêpe on a work surface and spread ¼ cup of the filling evenly over it. Roll the crêpe into a tight cylinder and place it, seam side down, in a 9-by-12-inch baking dish. Fill and roll the remaining crêpes. Bake for about 12 to 15 minutes, or until they are heated through but not dry.

Transfer the crêpes to warmed serving plates and spoon the remaining warm sauce over them and sprinkle with Parmesan. **Serves 4 to 6.**

Bannock: A griddle cake made from oats and/or barley, flour, butter, and water. It was used in Scotland and northern England for centuries as communion bread. Also called oatcake.

Barley flour: Milled from barley grain, this is a dense flour with a nutty, malty flavor and a distinctive dark brown color. It is available in health food stores and specialty food shops.

Belgian waffle: A thick waffle made in a special iron with deep grids called a Belgian waffle iron. It is traditionally served with whipped cream and fresh strawberries. The term "Belgian" refers to the dish's resemblance to an old-fashioned Belgian wafer cookie made by pressing batter between two grids.

Blintz: Made from crêpes or similar pancake batter, blintzes are rolled with a sweet or savory filling; folded into a rectangle, and sautéed in butter until golden brown. This Eastern European dish is usually filled with farmer cheese or fruit and served with sour cream as a main course or dessert.

Blini: Russian in origin, these are small yeast-risen pancakes usually made with buckwheat flour and served with melted butter and caviar, or sour cream and smoked salmon.

Buckwheat flour: This flour is milled from the seeds of the buckwheat plant. It has an assertive, slightly pungent flavor and is a rich source of vitamins and minerals. It is available in health food stores and specialty food shops.

Blue cornmeal: The dried kernels of blue field corn, grown primarily in the Southwest, are sold whole or ground into cornmeal and are used for making tortillas, cornbread, and pancakes. They give foods a bluish-gray color.

Buttermilk: The soured milk product left after most or all the fat has been skimmed off whole milk. Originally, buttermilk was the milky residue left after cream was churned into butter. Today, it is made by adding bacterial cultures to pasteurized skim or part-skim milk. The cultures convert the milk sugar into lactic acid, producing a tart flavor and a smooth, creamy texture.

Crêpe: Ultrathin unleavened French pancakes, rolled or folded with a sweet or savory filling and served as a first course, main dish, or dessert. They are best made in a flat-bottomed pan with short flaring sides designed to allow the crêpe batter to spread evenly and cook quickly.

Griddle: A large, flat, heavy pan with a shallow rim used for cooking foods like pancakes, French toast, bacon, and eggs quickly and with a minimum of oil. The flat surface, usually cast iron or aluminum, conducts heat evenly and the shallow rim makes it easy to use a spatula.

Dutch babie: A large pancake made from a batter similar to that of Yorkshire pudding and baked in a skillet. It rises and puffs as it bakes, and the center remains soft and custardy. It is said to have originated in a Seattle restaurant.

Hoe cake: Popular in America in the nineteenth century, this is a thick pancake made from cornmeal, eggs, flour, and butter. It is said that field workers used to cook the cakes on the blade of a hoe over an open fire, hence the name.

Johnnycake: In the 1600s, a johnnycake was a delicate cornmeal pancake made exclusively with cornmeal milled from Rhode Island White Cap corn. The seeds for this corn were handed down from the Narraganset Indians to Colonial settlers and are still being milled today. "Johnnycake" has become a generic term for any pancake, fritter, or bread made with cornmeal.

Latke: Jewish in origin, this potato pancake is made with grated potato, eggs, onion, matzo meal or flour, and seasonings. It is sautéed until crisp and golden and served with sour cream and applesauce.

Maple syrup: The traditional American topping for pancakes and waffles, made from boiling the sap of maple trees. It is graded according to color: The palest is Fancy Grade or Grade AA; Grade A, Grade B, and Grade C are progressively darker and stronger in flavor.

Maple cream: A thicker maple syrup that is whipped until it is smooth and spreadable. Also called maple butter.

Maple-flavored syrup: A less-expensive version of pure maple syrup, made from a mixture of corn syrup and maple syrup.

Maple honey: Maple syrup boiled an extra long time until most of the liquid has evaporated and it is similar in consistency to honey.

Maple sugar: A very sweet product made by boiling the maple tree sap until all the liquid is evaporated.

Sorghum syrup: Also called sorghum molasses, this is a sweet syrup made from the crushed stalks of sorghum grass. Its juices are rendered and boiled to produce a syrup similar to molasses but lighter in taste and color.

Sourdough starter: When a mixture of flour and water and sometimes a sweetener such as sugar or honey is left to ferment in a warm place, airborne yeast converts the sugar and starches into carbon dioxide gas. The result is a pleasantly sour-tasting leavening agent, used in yeast and quick-bread batters. This living culture can be kept alive indefinitely if it is replenished regularly with equal parts flour and water.

Swedish pancake: A small, slightly sweet pancake made in a large cast-iron griddle containing seven small, shallow depressions. The pancakes are traditionally eaten with butter, sugar, and lingonberry sauce or preserves.

Waffle iron: A hinged cooking utensil containing a cast aluminum or nonstick grid on each side producing a distinctive honeycomb pattern. Waffle irons can be electric or designed for stovetop cooking and come in several shapes including round, square, rectanglular, and heart-shaped.

WAFFLE AND PANCAKE COOKING TIPS

Consistency: If a batter is too thick, it won't spread enough on the griddle. To thin it, add a small amount of milk; then add more if necessary, but do not exceed ¼ cup. A thin batter will spread too much on the griddle. To thicken it, sift a small amount of flour over the batter and gently fold it in; add more flour if necessary, but do not exceed ¼ cup. Be careful not to overmix.

Storing batter: Pancake batter can be made the night before, covered with plastic wrap, and stored in the refrigerator. Stir it gently before using. Waffle batter can be stored the same way, but if the recipe calls for beaten egg whites, beat and fold them in just before baking.

Freezing and reheating: Wrap cooled baked waffles or pancakes individually in plastic, or layer between waxed paper. Place them in airtight plastic bags and freeze for up to one month.

To reheat pancakes, unwrap them, then loosely rewrap them in foil. Place in a 350°F oven for 5 to 10 minutes, or until heated through.

To reheat waffles, unwrap them and place them directly on the rack in a 350°F oven for 5 to 10 minutes, or until heated and slightly crisp.

Toasters and toaster ovens also work well for reheating. Microwave ovens tend to toughen waffles and pancakes and are not recommended.

Converting batters: All the waffle batters in this book can be made into pancakes without changing the recipes. With the exception of crêpes, blini, blintzes, vegetable pancakes, and baked pancakes, all the pancakes can be made into waffles. To keep them from being too heavy, separate the eggs and add the yolks to the batter. Beat the egg whites until stiff peaks form, then fold them into the batter as the last step.

WEIGHTS

Ounces and Pounds	Metrics
¼ ounce ~~~~~~~~~~~~~~~	7 grams
⅓ ounce ~~~~~~~~~~~~~~~	10 grams
½ ounce ~~~~~~~~~~~~~~~	14 grams
1 ounce ~~~~~~~~~~~~~~~	28 grams
1½ ounces ~~~~~~~~~~~~~	42 grams
1¾ ounces ~~~~~~~~~~~~~	50 grams
2 ounces ~~~~~~~~~~~~~~	57 grams
3 ounces ~~~~~~~~~~~~~~	85 grams
3½ ounces ~~~~~~~~~~~~~	100 grams
4 ounces (¼ pound) ~~~~~~~	114 grams
6 ounces ~~~~~~~~~~~~~~	170 grams
8 ounces (½ pound) ~~~~~~	227 grams
9 ounces ~~~~~~~~~~~~~~	250 grams
16 ounces (1 pound) ~~~~~~	464 grams

LIQUID MEASURES

tsp.: teaspoon
Tbs.: tablespoon

Spoons and Cups	Metric Equivalents
¼ tsp. ~~~~~~~~~~~~~~	1.23 milliliters
½ tsp. ~~~~~~~~~~~~~~	2.5 milliliters
¾ tsp. ~~~~~~~~~~~~~~	3.7 milliliters
1 tsp. ~~~~~~~~~~~~~~	5 milliliters
1 dessertspoon ~~~~~~~~	10 milliliters
1 Tbs. (3 tsp.) ~~~~~~~~	15 milliliters
2 Tbs. (1 ounce) ~~~~~~~	30 milliliters
¼ cup ~~~~~~~~~~~~~	60 milliliters
⅓ cup ~~~~~~~~~~~~~	80 milliliters
½ cup ~~~~~~~~~~~~~	120 milliliters
⅔ cup ~~~~~~~~~~~~~	160 milliliters
¾ cup ~~~~~~~~~~~~~	180 milliliters
1 cup (8 ounces) ~~~~~~~	240 milliliters
2 cups (1 pint) ~~~~~~~~	480 milliliters
3 cups ~~~~~~~~~~~~~	720 milliliters
4 cups (1 quart) ~~~~~~~	1 liter
4 quarts (1 gallon) ~~~~~	3¾ liters

TEMPERATURES

°F (Fahrenheit)	°C (Centigrade or Celsius)
32 (water freezes) ~~~~~~~~~~~	0
200 ~~~~~~~~~~~~~~~~~~~~	95
212 (water boils) ~~~~~~~~~~~	100
250 ~~~~~~~~~~~~~~~~~~~~	120
275 ~~~~~~~~~~~~~~~~~~~~	135
300 (slow oven) ~~~~~~~~~~~~	150
325 ~~~~~~~~~~~~~~~~~~~~	160
350 (moderate oven) ~~~~~~~~~	175
375 ~~~~~~~~~~~~~~~~~~~~	190
400 (hot oven) ~~~~~~~~~~~~~	205
425 ~~~~~~~~~~~~~~~~~~~~	220
450 (very hot oven) ~~~~~~~~~	232
475 ~~~~~~~~~~~~~~~~~~~~	245
500 (extremely hot oven) ~~~~~~	260

LENGTH

U.S. Measurements	Metric Equivalents
⅛ inch ~~~~~~~~~~~~~~~	3mm
¼ inch ~~~~~~~~~~~~~~~	6mm
⅜ inch ~~~~~~~~~~~~~~~	1 cm
½ inch ~~~~~~~~~~~~~~~	1.2 cm
¾ inch ~~~~~~~~~~~~~~~	2 cm
1 inch ~~~~~~~~~~~~~~~	2.5 cm
1¼ inches ~~~~~~~~~~~~~	3.1 cm
1½ inches ~~~~~~~~~~~~~	3.7 cm
2 inches ~~~~~~~~~~~~~~	5 cm
3 inches ~~~~~~~~~~~~~~	7.5 cm
4 inches ~~~~~~~~~~~~~~	10 cm
5 inches ~~~~~~~~~~~~~~	12.5 cm

APPROXIMATE EQUIVALENTS

1 kilo is slightly more than 2 pounds
1 liter is slightly more than 1 quart
1 meter is slightly over 3 feet
1 centimeter is approximately ⅜ inch

INDEX